SAKAMOTO'S SWIM CLUB

For Jim, who believed — J.A.

For Grandma Irene — C.S.

With special thanks to Coach Keith Arakaki of the Hawaii Swimming Club,

Nelson Okino of the Japanese Cultural Center of Hawaii,

Holly Buland of the Alexander & Baldwin Sugar Museum and Kai Duponte.

Published in Canada and the U.S. by Kids Can Press Ltd.
25 Dockside Drive, Toronto, ON M5A 0B5

Kids Can Press is a Corus Entertainment Inc. company

www.kidscanpress.com

The artwork in this book was rendered digitally in Photoshop.
The text is set in Colby.

Edited by Jennifer Stokes
Designed by Marie Bartholomew

Printed and bound in Shenzhen,
China, in 10/2020 by Imago.

FSC
www.fsc.org
MIX
Paper from
responsible sources
FSC® C005748

CM 21 0 9 8 7 6 5 4 3 2 1

Library and Archives Canada Cataloguing in Publication

Title: Sakamoto's swim club : how a teacher led an unlikely team to victory / written by Julie Abery ; illustrated by Chris Sasaki.

Names: Abery, Julie, author. | Sasaki, Chris (Illustrator), illustrator.

Identifiers: Canadiana 20200227165 | ISBN 9781525300318 (hardcover)

Subjects: LCSH: Sakamoto, Soichi, 1906–1997 — Juvenile literature. | LCSH: Swim teams — Hawaii — Maui — History — Juvenile literature. | LCSH: Swimming — Hawaii — Maui — History — Juvenile literature.

Classification: LCC GV838.4.U6 A23 2021 | DDC j797.2/1096921 — dc23

Kids Can Press gratefully acknowledges that the land on which our office is located is the traditional territory of many nations, including the Mississaugas of the Credit, the Anishnabeg, the Chippewa, the Haudenosaunee and the Wendat peoples and is now home to many diverse First Nations, Inuit and Métis peoples.

We thank the Government of Ontario, through Ontario Creates; the Ontario Arts Council; the Canada Council for the Arts; and the Government of Canada for supporting our publishing activity.

SAKAMOTO'S SWIM CLUB
HOW A TEACHER LED AN UNLIKELY TEAM TO VICTORY

Written by JULIE ABERY

Illustrated by CHRIS SASAKI

Kids Can Press

Preface

Who would believe that children cooling off in the irrigation ditches of sugar plantations on the Hawaiian island of Maui could become Olympic swimming champions?

Science teacher Soichi Sakamoto believed. He was determined to make a difference in their lives. With Sakamoto's guidance, Maui's swimmers surged onto the national scene and dominated events both in the United States and across the world. This included two Olympic gold medals won by Bill Smith in the 1948 London games.

Almost lost to history, the story of Sakamoto's swim club is an inspiration to athletes around the world.

Valley Isle.
Lush terrain.
Migrant workers
cutting cane.

Dawn to dusk
they toil away.
Children left
alone to play.

Melting in the
midday sun,
diving, swimming,
having fun.

Run!
Policeman's on his beat.
Children scatter
in the heat.

Sakamoto
takes a stand,
offering a
guiding hand.

He makes the case
for kids to train,
using ditch as
swimming lane.

Daily program.
Strict regime.
Use resistance.
Swim upstream.

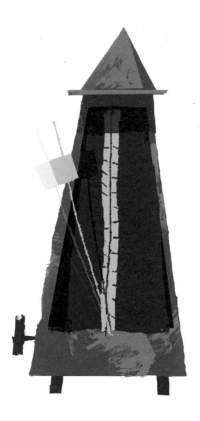

Science teacher's
new approach
turns him into
master coach.

Ditch to pool.

Plan is clearer.

Sakamoto's

dream grows nearer.

Swimmers share
Olympic dream.
Three-Year Swim Club
forms the team.

Make their entrance,
bright and loud.
Maui's swimmers
draw a crowd.

But tension knocks
at Europe's door.
Olympic hopes —
crushed by war.

Dawn raids shatter
peaceful skies.
Athletes answer
country's cries.

Dream awakes
in forty-eight.
Poised on blocks,
swimmers wait.

In the bleachers
full of pride,
Sakamoto's
tense inside.

Starting gun.

Bill dives clear.

Stroke by stroke,

he shows no fear.

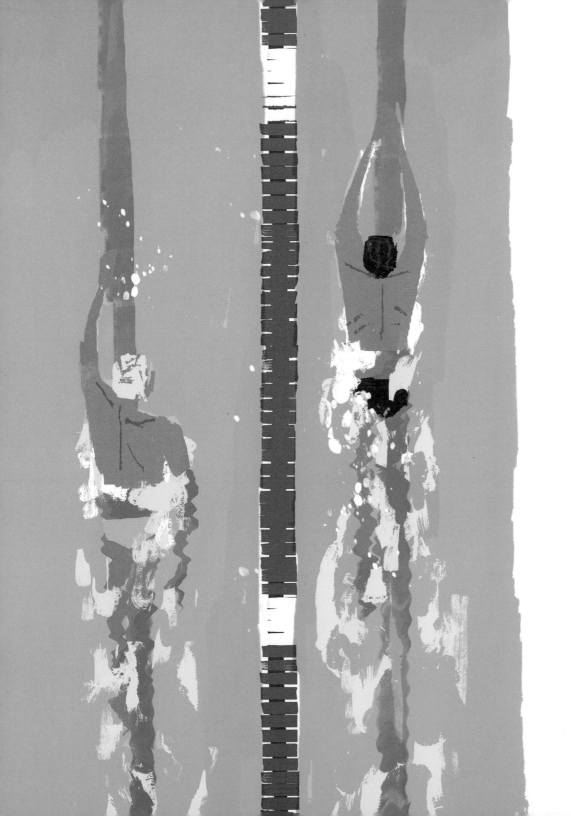

Pace, rhythm,
strength, speed
come together
to succeed.

Maui's swimmer
breaks the mold.

On the rostrum,
taking gold.

The anthem plays.
People cheer.
Sakamoto
wipes a tear.

Author's Note

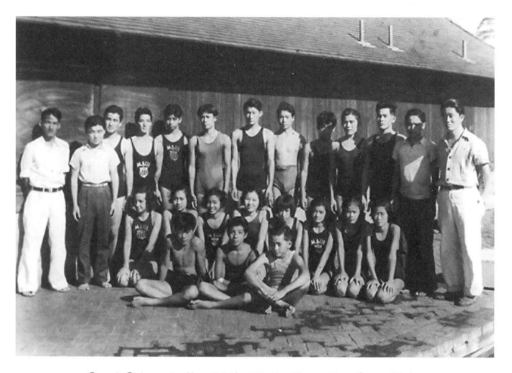

Coach Sakamoto (far right) with the Three-Year Swim Club.
From the collection of the Alexander & Baldwin Sugar Museum.

In Maui, also known as the Valley Isle, streams rush down lush mountain slopes. In the 1930s, water tumbled to the valley and flowed into irrigation ditches that nourished the island's sugar plantations. While workers toiled in the sugar cane fields, their children dipped and dived in the murky water of the ditches.

From his classroom window, a local science teacher named Soichi Sakamoto would watch the children swim. Then he would hear the clip-clopping of the plantation policeman's horse, and sigh as barefoot children scattered through the countryside to escape the officer's whip.

Sakamoto decided to speak to the owners of the Hawaiian Commercial and Sugar Company, offering to take responsibility for the children if the company would allow them to keep swimming in the irrigation ditches.

Every day after school, Sakamoto coached his ditch swimmers. Although not a good swimmer himself, he researched swimming strokes and applied his science background to come up with innovative training techniques. He ran alongside the kids, shouting instructions to improve their pace and rhythm, and used the water's natural current to increase their strength and speed. The swimmers learned to trust Sakamoto's coaching as their skills steadily improved. They worked hard each day, pushing themselves to swim better, faster and longer.

When the Hawaiian Commercial and Sugar Company built the community a pool and park, Sakamoto and his young charges spent every possible minute of every day training there. Sakamoto had a dream — and he would need his swimmers' commitment to make it come true. He called a meeting in his classroom. Would they agree to a tough three-year training schedule to compete at the 1940 Olympics?

That day, the Three-Year Swim Club was born. Their motto: Olympics first, Olympics always.

Maui's swimmers began to dominate at swim meets both in and out of the pool. They sported bright, colorful shirts, traditional straw hats and flower leis.

They entertained the press, singing Hawaiian songs with Sakamoto accompanying them on the ukulele. They were proud of their heritage. Their pride gave them strength.

Maui swimmers had never won a major championship, but, in 1939, Sakamoto's team surprised everyone by winning the National Championship in Detroit, Michigan. Now they were ready for the upcoming Olympics in Helsinki, Finland. But tensions were building in Europe and, in September 1939, World War II began. The Olympic Games were canceled.

When the United States entered the war in 1941, Coach Sakamoto watched many of his athletes bravely answer the call to serve their country. Like a father, he wrote letters to each of them.

Finally, in 1948 London, Sakamoto's impossible dream came true. Standing in the bleachers, with the crowd cheering wildly, the Three-Year Swim Club's own Bill Smith took a glorious win in the 400-meter freestyle race — an Olympic record and Olympic gold!

Affectionately known as Coach to his team, Sakamoto's legacy continued, with many of his swimmers going on to achieve national and international success, including more Olympic medals in 1952 and 1956. Sakamoto dedicated his life to mentoring hundreds of Hawaii's children. His goal was to make them the best they could be and give them opportunities for travel and education. Sakamoto was inducted into the International Swimming Hall of Fame in 1966.

Resources

Arakaki, K. "Missus." *Hawaii Swim*. May 1992.
http://www.hawaiiswim.org/legacy/hscMiss.html

"Coach Soichi Sakamoto." *Swimming Hall of Fame*.
http://www.hawaiiswim.org/legacy/coach.html

McQueen, Red. "World's Greatest Coach."
Ho'o mali mali column. 7 September 1941.
http://www.hawaiiswim.org/legacy/GreatCoach.html

Nakamura, Kelli Y. "Soichi Sakamoto and The Three-Year Swim Club:
The World's Greatest Swimming Coach."
The Hawaiian Journal of History, vol. 48, 2014.
https://evols.library.manoa.hawaii.edu/bitstream/10524/47254/1/1-Nakamura.pdf

Nakaso, Dan. "They promised to swim three years and beyond."
Adverstiser.
http://www.hawaiiswim.org/legacy/bunmei.html

Sakamoto, Soichi. "From the Tall Cane, Came His Champions."
JR/SR Swimmer Magazine. 1961.
http://www.hawaiiswim.org/legacy/tallcane.html

Tsukano, John. "I saw a dream come true …"
Honolulu Star Bulletin. April 1955.
http://www.hawaiiswim.org/legacy/Adream.html

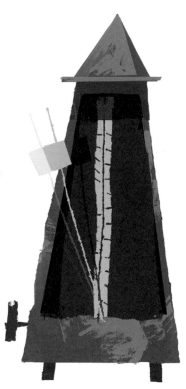